IT'S A DOG'S LIFE,
CHARLIE BROWN

Books by Charles M. Schulz

Peanuts®
More Peanuts®
Good Grief, More Peanuts®!
Good Ol' Charlie Brown
Snoopy
You're Out of Your Mind, Charlie Brown!
But We Love You, Charlie Brown
Peanuts® Revisited
Go Fly a Kite, Charlie Brown
Peanuts® Every Sunday
It's a Dog's Life, Charlie Brown
You Can't Win, Charlie Brown
Snoopy, Come Home
You Can Do It, Charlie Brown
We're Right Behind You, Charlie Brown
As You Like It, Charlie Brown
Sunday's Fun Day, Charlie Brown
You Need Help, Charlie Brown
Snoopy and The Red Baron
The Unsinkable Charlie Brown
You'll Flip, Charlie Brown
You're Something Else, Charlie Brown

Weekly Reader Books presents

IT'S A DOG'S LIFE, CHARLIE BROWN

A NEW *PEANUTS* BOOK

by Charles M. Schulz

HOLT, RINEHART AND WINSTON
New York • Chicago • San Francisco

ISBN: 0–03–030835–6

Printed in the United States of America

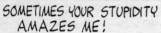

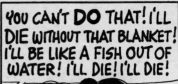

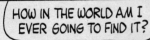

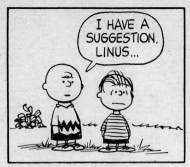

THERE'S ONLY ONE THING WRONG WITH THIS...

THE RAIN KEEPS RUNNING DOWN MY NOSE INTO MY EYES!

HERE'S A NICE PEBBLE, LINUS... TAKE IT HOME, AND OBSERVE IT..

THE FASCINATING THING ABOUT PEBBLES IS THEIR GROWTH, FOR SOME GROW UP TO BE STONES WHILE OTHERS GROW UP TO BE ROCKS...

YOU SHALL HOPE, OF COURSE, THAT IT GROWS UP TO BE A ROCK, FOR A PEBBLE THAT GROWS UP TO BE A STONE IS LIKE A YOUTH WHO HAS GONE ASTRAY!

✳SIGH✳ I HAVE SO MUCH TO LEARN!

"SOMETIMES HE WOULD STARTLE PEOPLE IN PUBLIC PLACES.."

"HE FLEW OUT IN ANGER AGAINST ALL THAT WAS PETTY, DULL OR GREEDY IN MEN"

"...OFTEN, HOWEVER, HIS SCORN WOULD TURN TO HIGH HILARITY AND HUMOROUS JESTS"

ARE YOU READING ABOUT BEETHOVEN OR MORT SAHL?

THE SUBJECT IS CLOSED, CHARLIE BROWN!

IT SIMPLY GOES WITHOUT SAYING THAT YOU ARE AN INFERIOR HUMAN BEING!

IF IT GOES WITHOUT SAYING, WHY DID YOU HAVE TO SAY IT?

THAT'S REALLY KIND OF DISILLUSIONING

WHAT'S THE MATTER?

SNOOPY ISN'T AS SMART AS I THOUGHT HE WAS...

HE MOVES HIS LIPS WHEN HE READS!

SCHULZ

DID YOU FILL OUT THAT PAPER FOR THE SCHOOL OFFICE?

I HAVE IT RIGHT HERE...

MY MOTHER'S NAME, MY FATHER'S NAME, OUR ADDRESS AND OUR TELEPHONE NUMBER...

WHAT DID YOU PUT DOWN UNDER "FAMILY PHYSICIAN"?

WELL, I WASN'T SURE SO I PUT DOWN "DR. SEUSS"!

SCHULZ

WOULD YOU CARE TO HEAR THE LETTER I GOT FROM MY PEN-PAL?

WELL, AS LONG AS I'M STANDING HERE, I MIGHT AS WELL LISTEN..

"DEAR CHARLES BROWN.... I THANK YOU FOR YOUR LATEST LETTER...IT WAS SO INTERESTING THAT I READ IT ALOUD TO OUR CLASS AT SCHOOL...."

"WE ALL AGREED THAT YOU MUST BE A VERY NICE PERSON, AND SOMEONE WHO IS PLEASANT TO KNOW."

HA!

"DENTISTS MOSTLY AGREE THAT THUMBSUCKING **CAN** AFFECT THE SHAPE OF THE TEETH AND JAW...**HOWEVER**...

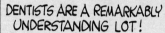
..DENTISTS FURTHER AGREE THAT PSYCHOLOGICAL IMPLICATIONS INVOLVED IN PREVENTATIVE STEPS TO CORRECT THE HABIT OF THUMBSUCKING FAR OUTWEIGH THE ORAL PROBLEMS."

DENTISTS ARE A REMARKABLY UNDERSTANDING LOT!

I AM ALWAYS IMPRESSED BY THE CONSTANCY OF THE STARS..

IT GIVES ME A FEELING OF SECURITY TO LOOK UP, AND KNOW THAT THE STAR I SEE WILL ALWAYS BE THERE, AND WILL...

THIS IS THE TIME OF YEAR WHEN I HAVE TO WORK THE HARDEST...

GETTING MY BASEBALL TEAM ORGANIZED IS A REAL JOB... THERE ARE A MILLION THINGS THAT HAVE TO BE DONE..

I HAVE TO NOTIFY ALL THE PLAYERS..I HAVE TO GATHER UP ALL THE EQUIPMENT..I EVEN HAVE TO SEE IF THE INFIELD NEEDS...

....MOWING!

SCHULZ

WELL, CHARLIE BROWN, HERE I AM READY TO START A NEW SEASON!

I'M VERY OPTIMISTIC ABOUT OUR CHANCES THIS YEAR, AND FULL OF ENTHUSIASM!!

BY THE WAY, ARE YOU GOING TO BE OUR MANAGER AGAIN?

YES, I GUESS I AM..

I'M VERY PESSIMISTIC ABOUT OUR CHANCES THIS YEAR, AND SUDDENLY I'VE LOST ALL MY ENTHUSIASM!

SCHULZ

I THOUGHT YOU SAID YOU WERE GONNA HIT 'EM **TO** ME?!!

I'LL BE ON YOUR TEAM, CHARLIE BROWN, IF YOU WON'T MAKE ME WEAR A CAP..

I DON'T LIKE TO WEAR A CAP BECAUSE IT COVERS UP MY HAIR...I HAVE NATURALLY CURLY HAIR, YOU KNOW

I DON'T SUPPOSE YOU'VE EVER HAD A PLAYER ON YOUR TEAM WHO HAS HAD NATURALLY CURLY HAIR, HAVE YOU, CHARLIE BROWN?

NO, BUT I'VE HAD MY SHARE OF OTHER PECULIAR KINDS!

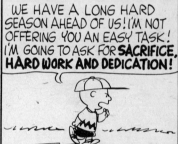

HEY, MANAGER..WE'RE AFRAID TO PUT OUR HANDS IN OUR GLOVES BECAUSE THERE MIGHT BE A SPIDER OR A BUG IN THERE!

OH, GOOD GRIEF! HOW DO THESE THINGS EVER GET STARTED?! HERE...LET ME PUT MY HAND IN FIRST JUST TO SHOW YOU THAT..

AAUGH!!

A BUG!

THANK YOU, MANAGER!

MONDAY IS OUR FIRST GAME, AND I FEEL LIKE LEAVING THE COUNTRY!

I'M JUST NOT CUT OUT TO BE A MANAGER, I GUESS......MY SHOULDERS AREN'T BROAD ENOUGH..

YOU MEAN YOU'RE NOT READY TO ASSUME THE "MANTLE OF RESPONSIBILITY"?

BEFORE IT WILL FIT **ME**, THE "MANTLE OF RESPONSIBILITY" WILL NEED CONSIDERABLE ALTERATION!

RATS! I'LL BET SHE WOULD HAVE BEEN SCARED IF I HAD **REALLY** BEEN DRACULA!

I WORRY ABOUT YOU, CHARLIE BROWN..

YES, I CAN IMAGINE!

NO, I REALLY DO

HAVE YOU HAD A PHYSICAL CHECK-UP LATELY?

I THINK YOUR FOREHEAD IS GETTING FAT!

WHOEVER INVENTED PORTABLE TELEVISIONS NEVER HAD AN OLDER SISTER!

SCHULZ

DEAR PENCIL PAL,
    WE HAVE A NEW GIRL IN OUR NEIGHBORHOOD. HER NAME IS FRIEDA, AND SHE HAS

NATURALLY CURLY HAIR

NATURALLY CURLY HAIR

THAT'S NOT WHAT I MEANT TO SAY!!!

SCHULZ

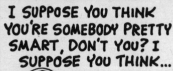

LET ME SEE THAT PICTURE AGAIN OF THE LITTLE GIRL PLAYING ON THE SOUTH LAWN OF THE WHITE HOUSE

YOU'RE RIGHT...SHE'S NOT HOLDING A BLANKET

OF COURSE, THERE COULD BE A REASON...

MAYBE HER FOLKS CAN'T AFFORD TO BUY HER ONE!

I'M WRITING A LETTER TO THAT LITTLE GIRL WHO PLAYS ON THE LAWN AT THE WHITE HOUSE..

I'M GOING TO OFFER TO SEND HER A BLANKET IF SHE THINKS SHE'D LIKE ONE...

DO YOU KNOW WHAT HER LAST NAME IS?

A CAT! A CAT!

SHE SAID SHE WAS GOING TO GET A CAT!

A CAT! A CAT! A CAT! A CAT! THIS IS DRIVING ME CRAZY! I'VE GOT TO TRY TO PUT IT OUT OF MY MIND!

IT CAN'T BE DONE! IT'S LIKE TRYING TO FORGET THE H-BOMB!

MAYBE I'M GETTING ALL WORKED UP OVER NOTHING..

MAYBE FRIEDA WILL GET A CUTE LITTLE KITTEN...AFTER ALL, KITTENS ARE A LOT OF FUN..

HA! WHY TRY TO FOOL MYSELF? IT WON'T BE A KITTEN....

IT'LL BE A BLAH CAT!

SCHULZ

SCHULZ

YOU? YOU ADMIT YOU WERE **WRONG?** YOU? YOU?!

OF COURSE CHARLIE BROWN.. AND I'LL ADMIT THAT I'VE BEEN WRONG BEFORE...

I REMEMBER THE LAST TIME I WAS WRONG ABOUT SOMETHING.. IT WAS IN 1958, I THINK... ALONG IN JULY SOMETIME, OR WAS IT IN AUGUST? YES!

THE LAST TIME I WAS WRONG WAS IN AUGUST, 1958.. I THINK IT WAS ON A MONDAY, AND...

OH, GOOD GRIEF!

SCHULZ

GOOD GRIEF! IT'S MORNING ALREADY?!

THIS IS THE DAY OF OUR FIRST GAME

I'M NO MANAGER...I CAN'T RUN A BASEBALL TEAM...EVERYBODY KNOWS I'M A LOUSY MANAGER... NOBODY EVEN PAYS ANY ATTENTION TO ME...THEY ALL HATE ME...

I THINK I'LL JUST STAY IN BED... MAYBE IT'LL RAIN...MAYBE NO ONE ELSE WILL SHOW UP EITHER.. I'LL JUST STAY IN BED, AND...

OKAY, MANAGER! RISE, AND SHINE!

I CAN'T GO OUT THERE TODAY, LUCY.. I'M NO GOOD AS A MANAGER...I'M SCARED!

SCARED? WHY, YOU BLOCKHEAD!

YOU WANTED TO BE THE MANAGER, AND YOU'RE GOING TO BE THE MANAGER! NOW, YOU GET OUT THERE AND MANAGE!!!

BOOT

HI, CHARLIE BROWN! WHERE HAVE YOU BEEN? WE'VE BEEN WAITING FOR YOU...

WELL, AT FIRST I THOUGHT I WOULDN'T BE ABLE TO MAKE IT, BUT I FINALLY GOT HERE UNDER THE INFLUENCE OF INFLUENCE!

PUNT!

I HAD NO IDEA THAT PUNTING COULD BE SO SOUL-SATISFYING!

THAT'S ODD...

LAST NIGHT I LEFT MY FOOTBALL IN THE BACK YARD, AND THIS MORNING IT'S IN THE **FRONT** YARD...

VERY PECULIAR...

THE "MAD PUNTER" STRIKES AGAIN!

PUNT!